T|

by Mark Stark

ISBN-10: 1539041034
ISBN-13: 978-1539041030

Dedicated to the explorer in all of us.

Part One

Sabbir,

Happy Travels!

Mark Star

The Beginning

The water shimmered like golden coins under the early morning sun. Ayama basked in the warmth letting it move inside and relax his body and mind. His breath deepened as he did so. Eyes closed, he could hear the gentle lapping of the Bay of Bengal waters on shore and the play of seagulls fighting over scraps.

It was the same this day and everyday he thought. Simple and good. Something to be appreciated. The ever-present sun provided a consistency, a nourishment. He spent much of his time alone and so viewed the sun as almost like a friend. Perhaps even as something a part of himself.

This was the spot Ayama came very early every morning when it was still dark out. The sand was cool on his feet but it was the coolness of the night that encouraged the fish to come closer to the surface. That was his opportunity to catch them.

Another machoarre, or Fisherman, had shared that idea with him. About getting to know the fish. A mysterious man, older than Ayama's seventeen years, who was hard to pin an age on but who would occasionally fish nearby and always seemed to catch a basketful without effort. The first time it happened Ayama stared in disbelief until the man looked over, smiling. This angered Ayama as his basket had one fish and he looked down at his rod like something was wrong with it. It was more of a stick really with fishing line he had fastened to the end and a hook at the end of the line.

"It's not about that," the Fisherman had called out.

Ayama didn't answer but could feel his anger dissipate. Like the salt scent from the water as it hit the air.

Over the recent months he saw the man at different times, often when he least expected it. Or when he thought he was alone. Like the morning before. On that morning Ayama had fished until the sun came up and the waters began warming as he sat on the rocky outcropping along the shore that was his spot. And as was so often the case was by himself. He could usually see one or two others fishing along the shore or on sitting poles out in the water a ways but now none were close by. And as he glanced over there he was. Within a stone's throw away the man stood along the outcropping, fishing line cast out into the waters. Not that it was easy to hear anyone over the water but it was like the man had come out of the waters.

Originally this had unsettled Ayama who was usually aware of what was around him. But over time he had grown used to it and even came to realize that there was something more to this Fisherman than his success with the fish. After all, his technique did not appear to be anything unique or special. Ayama had tried to copy his smooth, relaxed motions with the rod and pace but the fish he caught were fewer and the time he spent at the waters greater, not that he minded that. He enjoyed his time at the waters and had mainly taken up fishing as a source for a bit of food for himself and his uncle. Otherwise he would have spent time there anyway, gazing out to sea. Thinking. Reflecting.

He enjoyed the lazy way the day broke across the waters and land. He enjoyed the ritual of seeing the sadhus and bathers in the morning sun, playful dragonflies and damselflies whizzing about. He enjoyed the hypnotic ease of the doni boats that sailed out. He enjoyed the relative seclusion of this enclave as the men and boys with the nets and boats mainly used the harbor and coastal waters on the other side of the hill.

After the first encounter, they had shared a brief conversation in each of their meetings. And every time the Fisherman had made a comment that was like a seed planted in his mind for it had applied to more than just the fishing but to life in general. And in their last meeting Ayama had asked him if he was really talking about fishing or life and after a pause, a silence in which it was just the two of them and the water and dawn-breaking sky, the Fisherman replied:

"For those who are ready the world becomes a different place. The universe opens up and it holds nothing back. And why should it?"

Ayama did not have an answer. As was the Fisherman's way of making a point with a question which utterly served to silence him at the time. But he could feel the movement inside himself to explore the topic and ideas more. He desired that. At the time his mind was slow to grasp or respond as in a usual conversation but despite the lapses in days and weeks between their meetings he felt like there was a continuity to their interactions. Like time was not a distance or space at all but a mere pause.

In much the same way Ayama had viewed his existence up to this point. As a series of moments. He was mature for his age, sure. Used to doing things on his own. His light brown skin thickened from his time spent outdoors in the elements. The sun and coastal wind. His earliest memories were of his uncle and growing up in the hamlet his uncle had raised him with a loose hand, allowing him to choose his own direction at every point. Ayama never had the structure of the other children he had known but knew his uncle loved him. Ayama knew he was free to live as he pleased and that was his life up to this point.

He gripped the wooden hand cut pole in his hands as something tangible to grasp onto. Something in the Fisherman's presence and words spoke to him directly. Hinting at something much deeper. A depth even more vast than the expanse of azure waters he gazed out across. He was at once attracted to something... (what was it exactly?) And there was something unhinging about what he sensed the Fisherman was hinting at. Directions and possibilities they could have taken in conversation if he had only spoken out. He vowed to himself he would not stop himself from speaking what he wanted, despite the wall of fear that he could feel encroaching and limiting their interactions. He knew there was something, a great something he could learn from him.

And that is why this morning when the Fisherman appeared nearby Ayama did not wait. He lead his line in the water over to speaking distance with him and unashamedly spoke.

"Teach me what you know. I will listen and learn and be your student."

The Fisherman unhurriedly glanced over.

"What do you wish to learn?"

"Teach me how to fish like you. Teach me what you know about the larger things. About life."

"Isn't the fishing enough for you?"

"No."

"The waters, the fish, the experience. Everything is here this moment. There's nothing that is not here. Do you know that?"

And there it was again. A question that stopped him. He reminded himself of his promise and pushed through the lack of clarity in his mind.

"I feel that yes. But I know there's much that I don't know. And I desire to learn."

"Do you know how to read?"

"I can read enough. My uncle taught me. Books like 'The Old Man and the Sea' and 'Siddhartha'."

"Hemmingway and Hesse?"

Ayama nodded. The Fisherman cast his line out with an easy flick of his arm.

"And what have you learned from such books?"

"I am young in years but I know enough to see that books are only books. They can't really teach me what I want to know."

"And what is it you wish to know?"

"I can't say it in words. Something I've been looking for all my life. Something... more"

"And where do you think this something is? This 'something more' you're searching for?"

"You wouldn't be asking the questions if you didn't have the answers."

"Yes, but what's more important, to have the answers or to ask the questions? The answer to every question is inherent within the question itself. Is it not?"

"I don't know"

"Well, ask a question. Make it a big one."

Ayama stood there thinking.

"You're in your head. That is what stops you. The head is useful but it has its limits. And it interferes. Go ahead Ayama. Get out of your head. Ask a question."

"How did you know my name?"

"Now that's a question. Is your name a secret? Have you been hiding it?"

"No."

"It's an interesting thing. There's nothing that anyone can really hide from anyone else in existence. Not really. But people try, don't they?" he laughed. "The games people play are many. And they are fun games but they are distractions."

"Distractions from what?"

"Well, that's what you'll be learning now Ayama."

"You'll teach me then?"

"You have asked and I am here."

Ayama extended his hand and they shook.

"Now not so much talking. We might scare the fish away."

Ayama grinned and cast his line. Together they fished in silence.

The Opening

Ayama awoke from a nap in the early afternoon and asked himself if he had dreamt this morning or had it actually happened. He remembered asking the Fisherman his name and the strange reply.

"Call me what you will."

"What do others call you?"

"What others?"

"The people in your life."

The Fisherman looked at Ayama. Ayama could feel the warmth from him. An openness. A fearlessness. He had always felt a sense of trust towards him, knowing that even though he did not know him that he was safe. There was something familiar about him that he couldn't quite figure out. Maybe he did know him. On some level.

They did not look alike. Early on he noticed the light of the stranger's green eyes. His skin was slightly lighter than his own. Hair a light brown and longer than his cropped cut. A prominent nose and chin, not chiseled but larger than his. He wondered if he was from another country although he couldn't place the accent.

"Ayama, you could say I'm a traveler. People have called me by different names. I'm not being cryptic with you. It's just been a long time since I've stayed in one place."

Ayama realized it was not a dream. And the words "you have asked and I am here" repeated in his mind. Who was this man? He was unlike anyone else he had ever known, even the sadhus his uncle visited for their holy prayers and blessings. Could it be true that this man was answering something inside of him? Answering a question he did not even know that he had asked up until now?

Ayama pulled himself from bed and pulled on his plain t-shirt and shorts. His room was small and orderly, one of two small bedrooms. A handmade bamboo frame for the single bed against the wall and dresser opposite. A small window looking out on the gravel road below. A road leading to a small town center on the left and the coast to the right. The thatched roof dwelling was one of a series of connected one-story units. It was a simple hamlet with tea plants growing in the nearby hills and small boats in the harbor that would go out in the early morning darkness and come back mid-morning where the fishermen's loads would be sold fresh in the market square which featured a handful of shops and stands, a bakery and cafe and merchants who would spread their wares out for the day on a blanket or ground.

Ayama greeted his uncle with a kiss on his wrinkled forehead. He was seated on a cushion in the main room and looked up, cataracts in his eyes making him half-sighted. His uncle was a good-natured man approaching seventy. A man who had lived the hard life of a laborer but who stayed young in spirit and was quick to smile and laugh and see the good in life. It was just the two of them who lived together and it was that way for as long as Ayama could remember. And he always brought a smile to his uncle's face.

"How many fishies did you catch this morning Ayama, my boy?"

"One more than yesterday. So only three."

"Good, good."

His uncle's response every day to the same question, regardless of how many he had caught. When there was only a handful of fish they would eat it for meals or sometimes share with the neighbors. When there was more they traded it for goods in the market. Usually for baked goods, fruit and vegetables.

"You just missed Mia. Long morning?"

"You could say that."

He wanted to tell his uncle about the Traveler he had met but his uncle did not seem to care much about the larger things in life, the bigger picture, other than the few books they shared together but did not discuss. His uncle was content to live with what was in front of him and had lived a contented life. So Ayama thought another time perhaps. They ate together with the shared food on the mat between them: bread, nuts, fruit, hummus. Mostly in silence.

Afterwards Ayama walked down an adjacent road to visit his friend Mia who lived in a similar dwelling and was working on an old bike. She had it upside down and was working on the gears. Oil was on her hands and even a streak across her cheek but she didn't seem to mind. She was about the same age and his best friend. His only friend really and they had grown up together and were always close.

Ayama watched her at her work and they talked. About little and large things and everything in between. Sometimes in their conversations they invented fantastic stories which they told to each other or they would let their imagination free play and ask "What if...?" questions which usually ended in mutual laughter after things got too absurd.

The bike was about the same size as her slender frame but she expertly went about fixing it while listening intently to the story of the Traveler as he passed her tools. She looked up at him with her big brown expressive eyes and joyful smile.

"There are many holy and wise ones. On some city streets the sadhus are everywhere. The priests have their temples. The machoarre's are wise in their own ways."

"This one I'm telling you about fishes, yes. Better than all the others I've known. But I wouldn't call him a machoarre. He is something else."

"I am happy for you Ayama."

"Do you wish to meet him?"

"Maybe one day, if and when it happens. But this is your journey Ayama. I am here as your friend."

They continued in silence until the bike was in working order. Rust covered part of its body but it was a bike once more. She stood and looked down at it in satisfaction. Ayama took her for a ride on the handlebars down the gentle slope of the road.

The next morning the Traveler surprised Ayama by being first at the fishing spot. He was sitting on a rock dressed in his usual relaxed white-and-grey cotton clothes. No fishing pole or basket. Just himself. He invited Ayama to sit with him and Ayama put down his pole and they did so on the nearby sand. Ayama's fingers traced through the rough, pebbled sand where in the light of day the infinite fractures of little shells would soon glisten.

The Traveler did not speak. Just allowed Ayama to settle in the silence. Ayama could feel the strength of his gaze speak to him on a level without words. Like this was a prelude to something more. After a while he spoke and Ayama could sense the natural timing and flow of the words, like the ocean breeze drifting in.

"The sun shines, that is its nature. The eagle soars, that is its nature. The fish swims. The leopard hunts. The spider spins its web. The baby cries and giggles. The tea shrubs in these hills grow towards the light. The flower shares its essence, its fragrance and vulnerability. Not thinking of what it should do or be. It just does. That is its nature. What is your nature Ayama?"

"I am young and observe things. I watch and listen and hear what is around me, what people say to each other, how they treat each other and themselves. I have my life and it is what it is I guess."

"Yes you are observant Ayama. That much is clear. You have a sharp mind and see things the others don't. Simply because you choose to. You're aware of your surroundings, your environment, you feel connected to the water and way of life but desire for more as you've said. And what have you observed about yourself?"

"What do you mean?"

"Well, do you listen to yourself?"

"I think I do. Sometimes."

"Good. Keep going in that direction. But are you willing to see right now that you don't listen to yourself all the time and that, in fact, you deny yourself much of the time don't you? You deny that larger part of yourself for fear that what you've come to know about yourself, up until now in your life, is simply not true. And to acknowledge that would be really scary, wouldn't it?"

"I guess so."

"I guess so? Go inside yourself right now and ask if what I'm saying is untrue."

Ayama takes a moment, "No, you're right. I have been scared of discovering more."

"Why?"

"Because it would mean nothing would be the same.

My life would change and be different."

"Yes. And it would also mean that you would be open to the universe and existence and would have to release control of your life, wouldn't you?"

"Control of what?"

"Control of everything. Even at your age you have designed a life for yourself up until now the way it is and it is amazing and wonderful."

"I do appreciate everything in my life. My uncle and Mia and the townspeople and ocean and everything.

"Yes you do. And that's why we're having this conversation. Because you're ripe and hungry. For the 'more' that you mentioned. And giving up control of your life would mean not allowing your mind to dictate the course of your life anymore. For you would actively, consciously, use your mind to create your life and be what you want to be. To be what you are."

"Okay. So I try to control my life, try to control myself?"

"Yes."

"In what way exactly?"

"Well observe the way you do, but go a little deeper, from a neutral place. You see yourself as a young man who lives in this place with your life the way it's structured. The sun rises and sets. You are male and play a role, like everyone does. Granted you have more freedom than most in this game of roles. Your daily routine is one of habit for the most part. And you come down to the waters and judge yourself harshly for not catching as many fish as others, for instance."

"I guess."

"I guess?"

"Yes I do judge myself harshly. That is why I sometimes get angry when I see your basket full of fish?"

The Traveler nodded, saying nothing.

"And I guess I do judge myself in other ways. Like

when I think that I can't do something that I want to do. Like when Mia fixes the bikes and sells them in the market. I feel she is better at that than I would be and so I don't even start fixing bikes like her?"

"Even though…,"

"Even though that is something I might be really good at and she and I could do it together. Like in a business together."

"That's right! But that's only one possibility or probability. There are many others. Many, many others. You could say a million other choices and directions. It comes down to what do you choose, doesn't it?"

"So you're saying I control my life and so it keeps me in a certain place."

"Yes. And when you release control, then the possibilities open up. It's a matter of 'what would you like to explore?' For by nature you are an explorer, aren't you Ayama?"

"I grew up here and never really been anywhere else but I've always known there's more and that I wanted that in my life."

"Yes. And even though you've lived here all of your life, and you might continue to do so, if you choose. The difference will be that you will choose what you will and be aware of it now. Do you choose to live in awareness?"

"I do."

"And it's really quite that simple isn't it?"

"You mean just being aware of what I'm doing and what my choices are? Being aware of how I limit my life, and that I don't have to?"

The Traveler nodded. Ayama had spoken his thoughts and asked questions and allowed the conversation to develop and he felt a sense of pride in himself for his accomplishment. Like a job well done.

"And so this leads back to your question about 'What is my nature?'"

"Yes."

"I think I know what you're getting at. It's a lot to take in."

"It is. And that's fine."

They both gaze out at the ocean. The breeze sweeps onto shore and rushes against the palm trees and bushes.

"Can I ask you something?"

"Why not?

"Who are you? You're not really a fisherman, are you?" Ayama asks.

"Does it have to be limited to just one thing? See? That is the mind at work. Saying everything has a limit. I am that part of you that knows you are limitless and as such all of your creations are limitless. Look out to the ocean. See it stretch on to the horizon. And look inside yourself. Do you think it doesn't go even deeper and broader? Go inside yourself and see what's there."

After their talk they sat in silence on the sandy beach. The ocean flowed up the shore and retreated, back and forth. The moon was disappearing now and there was the faint pink glow of the sun rising just below the horizon.

After a while Ayama got up, brushed the sand from his body and sandals.

"Thank you."

The Traveler smiled.

"Don't forget your basket, Ayama."

And even though he had not used his fishing rod at all this morning, Ayama looked down to pick up the basket and to his great surprise it was heaped full of good-sized fish. More than he had ever caught in one day. He lifted his gaze from the basket but the Traveler was no longer there. He had disappeared in an instant.

Part Two

THE DOORWAY

It was two months before Ayama saw the Traveler again. On most mornings Ayama went to his fishing spot and expected to see him but he had never showed.

Their conversations played over and over in his mind. He thought about what his true nature was, of what it might be. He practiced listening to his inner voice and getting out of his head and being aware of just how much he had tried to control even his simple life. He more than thought about these things, he ventured to realize them and apply them to his life. To the point it became an ongoing practice. The practice of being aware. He did not yet know what it all had to do with fishing yet but he knew there was something he was missing. The proof was in his morning catches which were the same. Not many.

But more than anything Ayama puzzled over what he had seen when he last saw the Traveler. It was amazing! Unbelievable. It puzzled him to no end and his curiosity only grew the more he thought of it. It must have been a miracle for that many fishes to come from nowhere and fill his basket. For the Traveler did not have anything to hide the fishes in and he was with him all the time. No, it was not physically possible to fill a basket with fish like that, in an instant. It was a miracle he had decided and he was witness to it!

He had told his uncle and Mia about the Traveler and what they had talked about and what he had seen. They did not know what to think but they all agreed there was something special about the Traveler. His uncle shared something he had never known before: the meaning of Ayama's name which meant *"does not die"* or *"cannot be controlled"*. He had found that on the back of a baby picture when he had adopted Ayama as a baby, after his parents had died.

And when Ayama did see the Traveler again it was not at the shore. It was in the nearby town market. Ayama was there to buy some spices for his uncle (who did most of the cooking). He noticed the Traveler and they greeted.

"I wasn't sure if we'd ever meet again."

"Of course we were. What's a few months between friends?" The Traveler replied as he bit into a peeled lychee from the market. "How goes the exploration?"

Ayama animatedly filled him in on everything. He did not care to curb his excitement and at the end of it he blurts out:

"...And what was that all about? How did you do that with the fishes? How did you disappear like that? Like you always do! Is it magic?"

The Traveler grinned and gestured to a nearby clearing on a small mound where they sat.

"Well, since reality is an illusion, you could call it that. But it wasn't like a magician's trick."

"So it was a miracle?"

"Miracles are nothing special. What you saw was just the manipulation of energy. One based on the abundance of what you might call universal energy. What people call miracles is actually just the nature of reality, the way things really are. Beyond humanity's current understanding. A "miracle" represents the edge of your belief systems."

"So when you say you manipulated energy to create

the fishes... that is something I could do?"

"Of course."

"How?"

"First it's important to understand what energy is. *You are energy.* Energy is everything that is. Everything. That includes what we see, touch, smell, hear, and feel and everything else. It's the trees, people, buildings and everything in our environment. All that we perceive is a perception or interpretation of energy. A thought is energy. Desire is energy. A perspective of time is energy. Ideas of past and future or relationships, all of these are judgements of energy. Granted, it's energy judged and reduced through the filters of our minds but it's still energy. Does this make sense to you?"

"I think so. So everything that moves is energy and everything that doesn't move as well is energy?"

"Yes that's right. Everything. That's simplicity itself. Now stay with me for a moment. Everything is energy and all energy has consciousness, is consciousness. If the particles of a wall were vibrating at a different rate you would perceive it as something else, water perhaps, and be able to put your hand through it or walk through. You can call this energy whatever you want as it will be judged. It doesn't matter what name you give it really. Some call it ch'i, qi, prana, atomic, etc. Love energy or simply love."

"Okay. I follow what you are saying."

"Good. Now this is the important part. Going deeper with this idea. It's not enough to say that everything is energy and leave it at that. So what does this all mean to you? What would you like it to mean, Ayama?"

Ayama could feel the wall of fear rising again, threatening to shut down his ability to think clearly and express himself. At the same time, he could feel the big space of potential this whole idea of energy represented and wanted to play with that. To go into it.

"Well if I am energy... then that means I can do things like fill my basket with fish like you and do what I want."

"Sure but don't get hung up on that. Creating things out of thin air is not the important thing at all. Just because I skipped the usual steps in the creation process doesn't mean anything. Once we move into the awareness that the universe is energy then it becomes easier to see and to truly know and appreciate that we ourselves are energy. We are the creative energy essence of existence and can mold or shape energy into any form we choose. Look at how you've done it so far in your life. We can shape and create our life to be what it will. We can manifest our talents and abilities in their fullness and more. We can create and choose in any direction and follow the flow of this energy into any new direction at any point. We can re-frame or explore perspectives and beliefs or any concept. We can explore our sufficiency and true wealth within existence, as existence. We can live from a timeless, limitless perspective and more, not contraction or reduction. We can move beyond 3rd dimensional reality into the inter-dimensionality of existence. Energy is all things and the universe will allow everything. But let's not get ahead of ourselves at this point. Do you have any questions?"

"So why did you fill my basket with fish if it's not important?"

"Well it wasn't necessary of course but it did serve a minor purpose or two. To give your mind a direction of what is possible, to challenge your ingrained belief systems a bit. And to show you that there is abundance in the universe. Nothing is lacking. "

"So what's stopping me from holding out my hand like this..." Ayama holds out a perfectly flat hand. "...and creating an apple out of thin air? You're saying it's possible, I've seen you do it. Yet I've tried and I'm not doing it."

"At this point Ayama you're still playing with the idea of what we've been discussing. You don't yet know it within yourself to be true that you are energy. You still see yourself as separate from that which you wish to create, in this case an apple. You see yourself as separate from everything around you. Including that which I am."

"I guess I do. But I will work on it. Day and night."

The Traveler laughs, "Have fun with it by all means. Remember that by engaging your sense of awareness and seeing everything as energy does open you to the possibility of creating new things in your life. It will open you more to what is around you, how the energy is flowing and what is ripe for you to allow into your life, easily and effortlessly. It will open you to new choices and probabilities which will lead you in the direction of other choices, as I've said. It will open you to a limitless perspective of existence and your connection with everything. These are just possibilities when we get in touch with our true nature. There are no limits once we expand our awareness and begin to play with this as it's a new way of living and being. A new way of seeing. It's the empowerment of you. Imagine yourself unfettered and unshackled, truly empowered and in command of your existence. Move with the energy of who you are and start making choices that reflect this deeper knowing of who you are."

"And so this all ties in with observing everything neutrally?"

"Yes, observation *without* judgement. That is essential as otherwise you'll be stuck within a very limited perspective of things. A bubble. That's how people normally live. You've begun to open yourself up more than most but this applies to everyone. Take for example your physicality. We're sitting here and you perceive that we have physical bodies. Everything in your life is viewed from the perspective of your physicality. Think about it for a minute. Our bodies. Our interactions with others and our environment. The necessity for food, water, air, shelter, clothing. Sickness, health, well-being. Philosophy and religion. Movement. Cause and effect. Time, space. All of these things exist because of your physicality. But what happens when we open to a different perspective, a new perspective, one of energy? What begins to happen to our relationship with all of these things? When you choose – and the word 'choose' is key here – when you choose to see yourself as energy, as awareness, then everything opens up. Everything. Call it what you want."

"So energy is abundance?"

"You could say that."

"I spend so much time walking and by the waters. The sky is so vast and ocean so deep. At night the stars are there and it's clear to me at least that there's so much out there. So much."

"Look as far as you can see. Look to the horizon. Look to the stars and galaxies above. Look within the most advanced microscope and particles within particles within the atomic structure of your physicality. Gaze upon your life. See how you live and the choices you make. See it for what it is. See everything around you. The movement and stillness and form and space of everything. Even the perspective you have of how time affects your environment, your physicality. Observe your relationships. See how your choices create your interactions and relationships. See how your choices create your life. Now, do you really think that you are separate from anything? You cannot draw a line anywhere in existence and say 'This is energy, and this over here on this side is not.' Everything is energy. The energy that you are extends into everything. Such is your sufficiency. Open yourself up and explore what this means to you."

"So where does healing come into all this? I've heard about healers healing a sick person or animal. I know that is possible."

"Of course it is. Everything is possible. In what you call your reality here not all is probable but certainly healing is a definite possibility for those that go in that direction. Have you ever observed how a salamander or starfish can regrow parts of themselves? Have you ever paid attention to how many mammals and birds and insects have the capacity to communicate on a non-verbal level, telepathically, beyond what humans now allow themselves?

Have you ever observed how some things just flow into your existence without so much as a thought? How manifestation just happens? Have you ever observed your own body's innate capacity to replicate skin cells and the miracle of how it heals itself when cut or harmed? Do you honestly believe that the cells of your body were created with any inherent limits? Do you honestly believe that you have any limits? Scientists only ever discover the limits of their own bias. Their own perceptions. For how can they accept what they're not willing to observe and look at without their filters. Over time humans have adopted belief structures that reflect such limits. And they've done so for they fear their brilliance. They fear their beingness. Your body and cell structures have the capacity for infinite regeneration and rejuvenation. The Fountain of Youth is within. *It is your awareness of yourself as energy.* You are the master alchemist. Don't doubt what you're capable of, if only you gave yourself the chance."

Ayama found many of the ideas making sense but knew that his own understanding was only at the surface. He was not living any of it yet. He thanked the Traveler and they walked to the shore together in further conversation.

VULNERABILITY

Over the coming days Ayama spent time in meditation. Nothing fancy, just the simplicity of sitting in his room or by the ocean. Opening his mind and allowing everything he and the Traveler talked about to settle. He questioned some of the ideas more, for instance, the validity of the idea that everything was energy and found that it made sense. All of what the Traveler had said hinted at another truth, the ultimate oneness of things. That made sense to him, intellectually anyway, if energy was everywhere and everything than separation would be something we impose on things ourselves.

He shared his experience of the Traveler with Mia again and they discussed some of the ideas. She had an intuitive understanding of many of the concepts as well and did not seem surprised or overwhelmed. She did not seem as excited as him but was a good listener and he had always valued that in their friendship. When he sat with her as she repaired bikes he would look at her and try to see her and the bike as energy, rather than as a hard and fast physicality.

She would look up and laugh, knowing what he was up to. That would trigger his laughter. Things were always easy between them like that. Effortless and natural. She once commented that maybe the Traveler could fix the bikes by snapping his fingers instead of creating fish out of thin air. Ayama enjoyed her sense of humor.

Ayama noticed that he was more 'present' and aware throughout the day. When he sat with Mia or his uncle, he was there with them, not thinking of this or that and other things. He was choosing to engage what was right in front of him. He had always done so to some degree but his uncle used to joke that Ayama had been born to a pack of langur monkeys since he was not one to sit idle for too long and would cut a meal short and go walking or out to play with Mia.

About a month after his last meeting with the Traveler in the town market Ayama met him on the shores at their usual spot. The Traveler suddenly was there fishing, not twenty feet away, as if he had been there for hours. Ayama moved closer.

"Are they biting?" the Traveler asked without taking his eyes off the distance.

Ayama checked his empty basket. Noticing his sudden sense of frustration.

"Don't worry. All in good time."

"Easy for you to say." Ayama says.

"Something on your mind?"

Ayama pulled in the line and casted it out again. A little quicker than their usual pace.

"I think I get what we talked about. It makes sense to me. But my catches are no better than they were before. My life is the same. At least I think it is. Nothing is really different."

The Traveler turned and gazed at him. Ayama could feel the tightness of his body and grip on the pole relax and his energy soften.

"The outward appearance of your life may be what you've known it to be but do you really think for one second that there's been no change Ayama?"

"Well, meeting you is the big change in my life."

"Yes and didn't you choose to allow our interactions, our dialogue?

"Yes I have."

"And then realize that there is a movement within you. An expansion is taking place. You are opening to a greater realization of the way things are. You are opening to the realization of what you are. Are you not?"

"I am."

"That's significant. Recognize and appreciate that. For it will lead to many new and amazing new things for you."

"I've lived in this village for my whole life. I just feel frustrated. I want more and don't even know what I want beyond that."

"Ayama, may I ask you a question?"

Ayama nodded. The Traveler continued, "If you could be, do or create anything you've ever wanted in your life what it would it be?"

"I don't know."

"Go beyond what you think you can create. Go beyond the fear or guilt or hesitation. What are you most passionate about?"

"I've never really thought about it. I mean, moving into my awareness and what we talked about. Energy. I know there's a lot of possibilities."

"Yes there are and you're only beginning to explore them. Recognize that your mind is trying to control the exploration at this point. And that's okay. The mind is part of who you are, not an adversary, but it must be directed. You have observed how fear is part of your daily existence and it will continue to be part of your life. Until you reach a point where you realize what you are. Recognize that, more than anything else Ayama, what you are looking for is simply to manifest your brilliance all the time. And your brilliance is simply the expression of all that you are."

"How do I get there?"

"Recognize that you *are* that brilliance right now. Regardless of how you are choosing to manifest your life.

It's important to listen to that voice, that essence within, and get in touch with your vulnerability."

"Vulnerability? Like exposing myself to more?"

"It's not an 'exposing' as that definition of the word has always had a victim mentality behind it. There are no victims in the world, despite how things appear. Beyond the appearance of things there's only the energy of choice. And that is your empowerment. Your vulnerability is your power. Your vulnerability is your state of beingness. Beyond the mind's control. And initially that's a pretty scary place because it means opening yourself up to much more than you have before."

"And that's where I want to be?"

"Your life is a reflection of your choices. Moving into your vulnerability is a choice. Living in awareness and appreciation is a choice. Living from your beingness is a choice."

"A choice to not live in a shell."

"Right. A choice not to live in fear. To go beyond that."

"I think I'm afraid of what might be out there for me. Beyond this village. If I stayed here I could do what all the others do and live a life."

"Your life will go in whatever direction you choose. The form of your life can take on a great variety of manifestations. But recognize you're here for the journey. For the experience. And there's no need to play it safe and small. Doesn't everyone already do that?"

"Yes."

"And is that what you're interested in?"

"No."

"And by playing it small I'm not talking about living in a village or not but about the broadness of your perspective. The broadness of your choices. And the choice to be vulnerable."

"I'm interested in that."

"Good! Are you willing to open yourself, to be vulnerable?

"I think that's what I'm most passionate about.

About being honest with myself. Being real."

"I can see nothing else is really satisfying for you, is it?"

"If you are truly vulnerable then you're willing to choose freely without fear.   Vulnerability means letting everything happen and knowing you have the ability to move through it. And that is your power."

"Wow. That's a lot to explore."

"But that's the fun of it! Go explore and play and discover and be wild and free and laugh at it all. It's okay to laugh at what's taken as important and serious. Let's laugh at our pretensions and self-importance and be naked before the universe and it all."

Ayama smiled and cast his line out. He could feel it beginning. A journey taking him into a place where he always wanted to be. Already he could feel the energy of what the Traveler was talking about, as it applied to him and his life. And standing at the edge of the ocean waters was a perfect analogy for it. A jumping in.

THE ART OF ALLOWANCE

The next three months were the most difficult of Ayama's life. He had been excited by his talks with the Traveler and earnestly tried to apply what he had learned about energy and opening himself to existence. They were new concepts for him but they made sense and his direction was clear. For the first time in his life he felt that he was going somewhere, even though the destination did not have a name or location. Everything was starting to make sense and come together.

That was when his uncle became ill. Initially he saw a weakness in his uncle's steps and noticed he spent more time sleeping. Then the pain started and Ayama did his best to tend to his needs and make him as comfortable as possible. The doctor had come and gave his uncle some pills but it was serious and the doctor had taken Ayama aside and talked with him. The doctor was from a neighboring village and after an examination and tests informed Ayama that his uncle was dying and told him to prepare himself.

His uncle did his best to hide the pain from Ayama

but the way he breathed and winced communicated the situation. There was no family to assist them but the neighbors and village friends did bring food and dropped by occasionally. Mia was a source of comfort for them both. At first Ayama had forgotten about the teachings of the Traveler but a thought occurred to him: the teachings must be applicable to all life situations, the good and the bad, or what use were they to anyone? The idea made sense and he directed his mind to explore the concepts of energy and vulnerability and everything else. But it was not the same now. His uncle was dying and nothing else seemed to matter right now.

Ayama felt that if only the Traveler were there he could heal his uncle. He knew it was possible but where was he?

One afternoon Ayama fell asleep in the main room after his uncle had fallen asleep. He had drifted off to sleep in meditation with the intention of speaking with the Traveler. When he awoke the Traveler was sitting cross-legged on the floor facing him several feet away. It did not startle him.

"Am I dreaming?" he asked the Traveler.

The Traveler smiled warmly. "Your reality is a dream that you call real so you could say that. But no, I am here."

"My uncle is sick and needs your help."

"I cannot do that. I am sorry."

"But I've seen you do amazing things. I know you have the ability to heal him. I ask you to heal him. *Please!*"

"Healing is always possible. But it must be chosen by the person being healed. And not from the mind but every part of the self. And I do not see that your uncle will be making that choice."

"He will die. Are you telling me there's nothing we can do?"

"Everything has a process. And who is it for me or you or anyone to interfere in the process and journey of another. That would be an attempt to force or control, not honor and allow them their movement and choice within existence. Is that what you would want for your uncle, not to allow him to live his journey the way he is?"

"I just don't understand why he wouldn't want to live and be healed."

"What you call death is a part of life. The essence that is your uncle will never die but will choose to extend energy into a new manifestation of life. Another body. Another time and place. In fact, he already is alive this very moment. Incarnated as a young woman. A violin player."

"How's that possible?"

"Realize that we exist because on some deeper level we chose to be here. Not a choice from the ego-personality but the soul-essence level. Energy was extended to live and experience life from a particular environment and set of circumstances. Ayama, would you like me to show you?"

Ayama nodded and before his head was done moving the two of them were no longer in the house but standing at a city intersection. It was a lazy afternoon with nothing really happening. People were walking and enjoying a large public space nearby; some were reading on the steps which curved down to the flat of the main square.

Ayama was startled at first but quickly adjusted to the new environment.

"What just happened?"

"We took a quick trip."

"Where are we?"

"Downtown Portland, USA."

"You mean we are on the other side of the planet?" He looked over and the Traveler nodded.

"We just... teleported?"

"Yes."

"How?"

"A choice was simply allowed. Nothing complicated."

People walked through the square, including a slender fifteen-year old young brunette with a violin case. The Traveler made a gesture indicating she was the one he was talking about.

"She is my uncle?"

"No," the Traveler laughed softly. "But she is the same soul-essence as your uncle. The same energy. Do you see how it works now?"

"I'm starting to. So even though my uncle is dying and will be dead soon, he's really won't be dead?"

"Something like that."

"Okay. And we can move from one place to another just like that?"

"Yes."

"Why aren't others doing what you do? I don't see anyone else teleporting."

"There are a handful of others that come and go on this planet, but you're right. It's not a common thing."

"Why not?"

"Because you've forgotten what it means to simply allow. Humans were once in touch with their power and ability to create. A long time ago. But they've since given their power away. You can see it everywhere. In how they treat themselves and others. In how they use the land and technology. But that's for you to observe. It's for you to observe how you've given your own power away."

"And you've taken back your power?"

"To some degree, yes."

"So even you have not fully realized your power?"

"No. But in my life I've opened myself up, connected with my essence, the universal essence, and simply 'allowed' a little more than others. And the result is that I can do some things that you find... impossible."

"And this is what the other teachers and saints have done?"

"Some, yes. Like I said, to a degree. What do you think Jesus was doing when he turned water into wine? Do you doubt that this ability and more exists within you as well? My existence is a reflection of who I am and where I'm at. And it's only the beginning of what others will be and create. Like yourself."

"Me?" The Traveler nodded.

"So we can simply allow ourselves to be somewhere else?"

"Not just be somewhere else but you can explore time as well. One day your history books will look much different. They will all be re-written when it's discovered that there's much more to the past than currently understood. Look over the past decades of life on your planet and see how the future is being accelerated with new technology. Where do you think some of this technology has come from?"

"From someone moving through time?" The Traveler nodded.

"Wow. Okay, let me see if I got this. So, through allowance we can create anything?"

"Whatever you're willing to allow into your reality. You can manifest the energy that you are in any way. You can manifest it as property and physical things, as relationships, as lack, as movement, as new choices in your life. That which you are is much more than any one creation but is creative energy, the essence of energy and the All-That-Is. Play with your perspectives. Get in touch with your connection with all of existence. The choices you make ripple out into the world and universe and extend through time. They literally alter, and are, the fabric of existence."

"I'm trying to understand a bit more how this relates to my uncle dying."

"That's for you to come to terms with. Do you really feel that life ends when this body you have ceases to be? Do you believe in your heart that the essence and energy you are can ever cease to be? You are life without beginning or end. You are eternal - if you want to look at it from the judgement and filter of time. You are infinite. You are energy. And yes you are manifested here, in this time-space reality. But are you aware of all this? The limits you exist by do not change who you truly are. This life you are living, realize the theme of it is to experience and explore this idea of physicality and all that it entails. The intensity, density, limits and joy of it. This physicality is not the summation of life but only an extension and representation of that which you are. The energy and wonder and brilliance of you. So play with it and live large. Experience your empowerment and awakening. Realize the consciousness that made the choice and continues to choose to be here now in the form and perception of you as you define yourself to be. And realize what allows this choice."

"This idea of allowance is a lot more than I thought it was. That's a lot to grasp."

"Realize that the art of allowance is not just about allowing things that you want into your life. A new boat. Lots of fish. Money. A big house. That's part of it but allowance is about knowing that life happens. The energy of the universe takes shape and form, circumstances and situations arise. Sooner or later everything is manifest. The journey of life is like a roller coaster. Up and down. Events can happen in an instant that can alter and change your life. Allowance and vulnerability means you're willing to see that the illusion of this world has no real power over you. You can allow life to happen and not try to control anything."

"So you're saying it's possible to be at ease with my uncle's death? That I don't have to resist it but can look at it in a new way."

"That's right."

The Traveler and Ayama walked down the sidewalk at a leisurely pace and watched the young woman take out her violin from its case and play in the square. Passers-by enjoyed her playing and it was clear she had some talent and skill.

"You make it sound easy."

"It is easy. But people make it hard. They complicate and develop techniques and methodologies and create a 'process'.

"So process is related to time?"

"Of course. And that's fine. You're here in this dimension or reality and that's the way it is here."

"Until we move beyond it?"

"Yes and to move beyond technique and the endless trying in your life means to simply allow. To simply do it.

It's not a thought or process, although you can do it that way. But that's a complication. A mental process. Go into the simplicity and simply choose. Everything else is just a game. A game of disempowerment that humanity has become addicted to like TV and heroin. Simply do it. Make the choice. There's nothing to figure out. Between now and tomorrow your reality can change completely. But what are you willing to allow into your life? Do you not believe that the energy of the universe that creates the stars and planets and sustains all life will not support you in your choices? Get in touch with this energy, for you're not separate from it. It's your perception of separation that fuels and keeps you in your limitations."

"So I perceive my uncle dying as a bad thing and that's just the way I'm used to looking at things. But I can shift the way I'm looking at it. I can allow more into my life?"

"Of course. It's possible to reframe how you see any situation or circumstance and empower yourself. Realize that there's no separation of anything in existence. The world is your reflection, your playground. *Choice is your empowerment. And you are the energy of choice.* We accept some things into our lives. But what would it mean to accept everything the universe offers us? What would it mean to move with the ebb and flow of the universe and be a oneness with all that is? What would it mean to move beyond the dream that is your life and open to it all? What would it mean to be truly vulnerable in the moment you find yourself in? And where would that lead you?"

"Okay I get it."

"The universe is unfolding. The energy is moving and shifting and manifesting. We begin life and the energy of the universe flows through us. Observe the energy of a baby and see this. Look into their eyes. Infinite possibility. The same energy is within us in every moment. But how many allow it to manifest in their lives?"

"I love what you're saying and how you're saying it. And that's where I want to be. To have that clarity."

"Good! Be simple then. When you turn away from your simplicity you harm yourself. Explore possibility and probability and choose to lighten your life. Everything can become simple and the exploration changes to one of an expression of the ease of your energy. This is the art of allowance. Do you see how it ties in with the nature of your beingness?"

"Yes I think so. My beingness is who I am but it must be chosen if that's how I want to live."

"Yes you must choose your limitlessness and realize that you *are* possibility and choice. It's inherent in who you are. Inherent in your energy. That doesn't mean that you have to manifest in any one particular way at a given moment. That would be a game of control, not allowance. You were once a little boy or girl. You inhaled oxygen into your little lungs and stood open before the universe. This young woman playing the violin is realizing a choice she made a long time ago. A choice she continues to make. Open to magic and possibility. Open to life. What would you most like to explore and create in your life?"

And in an instant Ayama was back in the main room of his house. No Traveler, just himself. He took a deep breath and sat in silence for a while before going into his uncle's room. Ayama sat bedside and watched the movement of his uncle's chest as he slept. Listened to his shallow breathing. He was glad his uncle was able to sleep as at least he was not in pain then. In two days his uncle died and a small and simple funeral was held. At the funeral Mia held Ayama's hand and they embraced.

Even after his talk with the Traveler he was sad to see his uncle die but felt a deep sense of appreciation that Mia was with him. His uncle lived his life and was no longer there. But a part of Ayama could feel his energy and love.

Part Three

THE RIVER OF LIFE

In the days following his uncle's death Ayama lived alone in the house and continued his early morning fishing. His missed his uncle's smiles and humor and presence. Mia and Ayama spent more time together, often in silence. Sometimes they would walk in the countryside and talk. Inside himself Ayama felt that he was healing from the loss and finally coming back into life.

But the routine of fishing and way of village life was at once so much a part of him and yet he could feel himself at a crossroads. That perhaps the time had come to leave the town and go in a new direction. There was nothing really holding him there but his friendship with Mia. He loved her as his friend and more. But she had her family there and he did not want to ask her to leave them. In his uncle's passing Ayama had inherited the dwelling which wasn't much, but there was also a small amount of money that he could use to travel.

One mid-morning as he was about to leave the fishing spot the Traveler appeared. They looked at each other as friends and shared warm smiles. As was their usual custom.

"How goes the exploration Ayama?"

"I'm leaving the village. At least for a while. To see what else is out there."

"What do you have in mind?"

"I'm not sure. A new start. Wherever life takes me?"

"It sounds like you're open for something new. Good for you."

"What is this thing called 'life' all about? Why are we here really?"

"Simply to do what you're doing. To explore the experience of it all. The experience of existence."

"I've wanted to leave here for a while but was afraid."

"Don't be afraid. Consider your life and existence to be as one long river. Connecting with that greater movement and energy can be scary and exciting. It's a homecoming. Embrace the totality of that which you are."

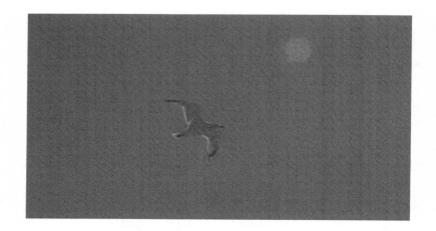

"That might take some time."

"It will but that's your choice. It doesn't have to take much of what you call 'time'. Connecting with your essence means opening to more of yourself. Beyond what you think or have come to believe is you. And that connection needs to be a deliberate, conscious choice. A choice at *every level* such that it is simply so. You will be that choice."

"And connecting with my essence I can live my life, make choices and be and do what I want."

"Of course. You're never stuck into one choice. You are free to keep choosing and living and exploring. There's no beginning or end to that which you are. Be and do whatever you want. Be a success. Be a failure. Be rich. Be poor. Be bold. Be timid. Be a sinner. Be a saint. Live long. Die young. Fly high. Live your life. Change how you see yourself. Make mistakes. It's all okay. It's more than okay. It's inevitable. And from one perspective there are no mistakes. We live and die and come back again and again and life can never be extinguished. The universe is big enough for it all. For all our choices and explorations.

Explore what's possible. You might surprise yourself. What would you like your life to be a reflection of?"

"I just want to be me. More of me. I don't feel I know what that is quite yet."

"You will. Very few actually do so you are going in the right direction, Ayama. Keep choosing and trusting yourself and living your truth. Appreciate your life and everything in it. Don't take anything too seriously. Remember when you were a boy or girl and used to look up to the sky and twirl around and fall to the ground all dizzy and joyful? Remember seeing the newness and wonder of it all and were exploring it, discovering where the boundaries were? Maybe it's time to explore and play again and to discover new boundaries and limits. Be in wonder again. Be joyful. Smile. Play. Laugh. Challenge yourself to see things in new ways. Walk barefoot in the water and grass. Greet a stranger like they were your best friend or share compliments more freely. Dare yourself to be a little crazy. You'll move through your existence in the way you will until a point is reached where you'll no longer deny yourself of the love you have for yourself and all existence. For in truth, the love that you are is the love of all things, and the love of all things is the love you are. This is the empowerment you are moving toward, the realization, the movement. All of your experiences and exploration in all of your lifetimes are leading you to an opening which will be the expansion of consciousness and awareness. And no stone or pebble will be left untouched or unturned."

"And we are all on this journey? Every person?"

"Yes. It's the journey back into oneness. And the oneness is more than the mind can grasp. Just realize that you are the journey and the journey is you. If you see yourself as separate from anything around you, then you'll never find the wealth and abundance that you desire and seek. For there isn't enough money or gold in the world to fill that hole, that perception, as it's one that'll fuel your perspectives of lack and insufficiency in your existence."

Ayama and the Traveler climbed the hill towards his home. "I know I've grown. But I feel a little dumb or slow right now. Not very conscious. What exactly is consciousness by the way?"

"Consciousness is the awareness of existence. It's the knowing that you are much, much more than what you've defined or limited yourself by. It's the realization that you exist beyond the physical, mental, emotional and spiritually manifested aspects of your existence, beyond any one particular defined circumstance or reality. When someone observes their life without judgment it becomes clear how their choices create the reality in which they exist. They become aware of the interconnection of their energy with all that exists and the choice is made to move with that energy, that movement and understanding. "

"That we are all the river of life?"

"Exactly. And then there's no longer a necessity or desire to see themselves as separate from anything since energy, no matter how you define it, is all that is. Realize that the reality in which you live is a reflection of your awareness. If you want to change it, simply do so. Every perspective or perception is a limitation of your awareness or level of consciousness. That includes the limits you've chosen to exist by such as death. Death defines so much about how we see ourselves and it seems to be the grand, inevitable and terminal conclusion to our lives on this planet. And such a serious and somber finality at that."

"So even death is just an idea we've adopted?"

"Yes. The idea of death is only a perspective or belief that can be moved beyond. It's an illusion like all other perceptions. You don't have to wait until your physical body ceases to be to explore what is beyond death. The realization that you are energy is this exploration, the movement beyond limitations. It's inevitable you will remember who you truly are, but why not do it in this lifetime? The idea of interconnection and oneness remains that – an idea – until your energy is extended into creating that reality through your choices. Some people in the spiritual circles have an intellectual grasp of the essence of existence, the oneness energy, call it what you will. But how many empower themselves to consciously choose it all the time and live from this state?"

"Not many I'm thinking."

Over tea at Ayama's home they continued talking. Ayama listens intently while the Traveler softly speaks:

"...the limitations created by the choices you make to perceive yourself and life a certain way, and then you say to yourself "this is how it is". And isn't this the way humans live? From green young saplings at birth to stiff brown branches within the span of not so many years. The hardening of the heart and perception in different ways. Remember times as a child when all you wanted to do was explore and play and have fun? Adults would tell you one thing and your first reaction to them would be "But that's silly!", an intuition and knowing from within. Over time people stop questioning things. They stop asking why. They stop taking that leap of faith into the unknown, the uncharted landscape of our inner world (and outer universe). We stop questioning what the mind perceives as fact or something that is obvious so why bother. It's our nature to question and grow and experience all that life is. Yet how easy it is to settle into "comfortable" lives until that irritant arrives. Perhaps it's a nagging dissatisfaction from within that something is not the way you truly want it to be. Something feels off or not in alignment in your life. Perhaps everything. Or perhaps you get hit by a big truck in the way the universe can deliver when we are not listening: disease or illness or death or tragedy happens. And our life is upended completely. Observe your life carefully... set the judgements aside and just simply see where your choices have lead you... be honest and see the influence that your judgements and fears have had on your life. And the fear of fear. Observe how people over time give up their red wagons and sand shovels and settle for adding machines and ledgers and schedules. People have stopped playing and being child-like."

"That's what I've always resisted. That slide into adulthood. I know children have so much to teach adults." Ayama adds.

"Of course. But observe the level of control you've exerted in your life Ayama... the worry and trying, the stress and effort and contraction. Breathe in deeply and relax. How many try to control their lives or use some idea of 'change' as a substitution for a real exploration and the movement into their beingness? Oftentimes people take up a new pursuit or sport, a new relationship or job, take a vacation or they change their clothes or look, or even shift into a slightly new way of thinking about themselves. But is this growth or just change? Have they let go of anything really or are they still operating from within the same paradigm that they're trying to shift out of? How satisfying is it living like that? When was the last time you took a truly deep breath and felt that sense of "Ahhhh. This is good!"

"Yes and I want that. To live that way. Every day."

"Good! Then observe closely the influence of your mind in your life and you will see the extent to which the mind interferes, limits, reduces and tries to control things as a way of 'surviving' and ensuring its continuity when it is not consciously directed. When you're not in your beingness. The result is quite crippling. And so through lifetimes there is only very small movement and shifts in awareness. Very little growth if any. And from one perspective that's okay but is it your choice? Is it what you really desire and want right now? The energy you are is one of love. It's one that opens and encompasses all things. It's a brilliance beyond compare. Take a moment to feel the truth of this statement and bring it into your life... Now, explore this beautiful idea: releasing control of your life and living from the awareness you have of your deeper self. Your energy and beingness. Let go of control and embrace the mystery and vastness of life.... of your own beingness. Your mind is always trying to solve the great puzzle of who you are. It attempts to define and measure and scrambles for answers and then spends so much time and energy justifying choices. This is what you do. It is what everyone does. But our beingness is undefinable. Inexhaustible."

"And so any answer or description of our beingness is not really it."

"Exactly. How liberating and freeing would it be to simply acknowledge that you can't control your life and that you don't have the answers to the puzzling? The illusion of control can be created but is that truly living or is it simply playing a game with yourself? When you explore your fears and the incessant striving of your existence, there's movement into a deeper understanding. The realization that you lack nothing. The space opens up for a more genuine and real exploration into new choices. Into growth and empowerment. Before you achieve the beingness that you seek, a letting go takes place. This is what you're here to explore and discover and take part in. To enjoy. You have a choice to make: to live your life from the shore or to jump in the water. To go play in the ocean. Rediscover your ability and talent to play and wonder and explore and love. Life is a treasure so go out and get wet."

"Maybe if I got wet I could catch more fish."

"Give it a try. See what happens." the Traveler said as they both laugh.

"I feel like I've been waiting for so long for something to happen. Anything. Maybe meeting you was what I was waiting for."

"What have you been waiting for? If you aren't alive in your life, living to the fullest and celebrating life then it's important to ask yourself why not? You don't need me. I'm merely helping you remember what you already know. Yes, we exist. And as humans we have these amazing tools called our minds with which we perceive our lives and reality. We create our lives through our choices and perceptions. And it's all too easy to slip into a state where we go through the motions of life, anticipating the future in a myriad of ways, or caught up on the past. Or just giving our power to something outside of ourselves and closing our hearts and minds to what is possible. When we are alive and experiencing life and ourselves to the fullest then we are choosing to invest ourselves in the moment. We are choosing to breathe and live and be, recognizing that we are worthy of the experience of joy and the abundance that is our birthright. The larger part of you known as your soul-essence chose to be here. Energy was extended into the world and the creation and experience that you call your life began. And more and more people are choosing to explore this area and re-awaken, allowing their essence and true self to manifest in the world. It is still a very rare thing in the world but people are slowly shifting into new directions. We experience life through many lifetimes and from one perspective it's all just experience. And we're here to experience the experience of existence, as I've said. In the ways we desire and create. In the ways we allow and choose. And eventually it's all experienced and everyone moves into a true understanding and awareness of themselves, but very few in any one particular lifetime. And if your choice is to live from your beingness Ayama then let it reflect out into the world as an example for others. For what is the reality you perceive but an extension of your own energy and a reflection of our own state of awareness? Extend your energy and play in the playground this world is! Living life fully is not about having material riches per se. I'm talking about the experience of the wealth that you are. That is endless wealth and the material riches of this world pale in comparison to that. There's not even a comparison. For your energy encompasses everything. We choose the degree we wish to be involved in life, with our jobs and relationships and interactions with everyone. With what is happening around us in whatever moment. In this moment. And it all begins with you. What is the degree you wish to know and consciously express your essence, the love you are? It's important to pause at times and ask yourself if you are ~alive~ or merely going through the motions and running on automatic pilot. A person who is alive knows it. As it feels like flying. It feels unlimited. And I'm not talking about the mind's idea of excitement but about the manifestation of your energy in to the world. Your brilliance is about the expression of all that you are. And there isn't really another word for it."

They drank the tea and talked more. After a while Ayama changed the tone.

"I feel like our talk today was a parting of the ways in a sense. Will I see you again?"

"You will. But it'll be down the road. There's much for you to explore. And more for us to explore together at some point, if you wish."

"When I'm ready."

"When you're ready. And when you are, our talks will be a little different."

"Can I ask...?" Ayama hesitates.

"Yes?"

"What do you see between Mia and me? Are we together in the future?"

"That's up to the two of you. Isn't it? But I do see that's likely the case. There's much for the two of you to explore and create together. What you share is something special. Something to be nurtured. Ayama, thank you for the tea."

The Traveler stands and walks to the door.

"Until our next meeting."

"Thank you."

And for once the Traveler exits in normal fashion, simply by walking out the door. Ayama does not bother to check and see if he is walking down the road.

He smiles and feels his sense of awareness. Feels his connection with the Traveler. Like they share an awareness.

In the closet of his bedroom is a worn shoulder bag. He fills it with a few clothes and leaves a note for Mia in the main room. And then Ayama, with nothing but the bag, glances back. Then leaves the house he grew up in.

About the Author

Mark Stark has been on a journey of self-discovery all of his life. He facilitiates healing and awareness shifts in others and is open to meeting people and new experiences.

His website is **www.theradiantself.wordpress.com**

If there is interest, future books in this series will share the journey of Ayama as he explores and grows and becomes a teacher himself. His connection with Mia will be a feature of the series, including one book subtitled **The Path of Love**.

61920262R00058